Inside the NFL

THE HOUSTON OILERS

BOB ITALIA

ABDO & Daughters

Published by Abdo & Daughters, 4940 Viking Drive, Suite 622, Edina, Minnesota 55435.

Printed in the United States.

Cover Photo credit: Wideworld/Allsport
Interior Photo credits: Wide World Photos, pages 4-8, 10-14, 16-19, 21, 22
Archive Photos, pages 23, 24, 27

Edited by Kal Gronvall

Library of Congress Cataloging-in-Publication

Italia, Bob, 1955—
The Houston Oilers / Bob Italia
p. cm. -- (Inside the NFL)
Includes index.
Summary: Describes the formation, history, and key players of the football team that has been one of the top teams in the NFL but has never made it past the second round of the playoffs.
ISBN 1-56239-551-3
1. Houston Oilers (football team)--history--juvenile literature. [1. Houston Oilers (football team). 2. Football--History.] I. Title. II. Series: Italia, Bob, 1955— Inside the NFL.
GV956.H68I83 1996
796.332'64'0976414 11--dc20 95-34987
CIP
AC

CONTENTS

Great Teams, No Titles

In the late 1980s and early 1990s, the Houston Oilers were one of the top teams in the National Football League (NFL). They made the playoffs six straight years. They had one of the NFL's best quarterbacks in Warren Moon. Their wide receivers terrorized opposing defenses. And their own defense was one of the toughest in the league.

From 1975 to 1980, coach Bum Phillips led the Oilers to five winning seasons, two divisional titles, and two AFC championship games.

Yet despite their potent offense and rock-solid defense, the Oilers could never make it past the second round of the playoffs. Frustrated with their dismal playoff record, management grew impatient and traded away the heart and soul of the team—Warren Moon. The following year, the Oilers fell to the bottom of the AFC Central Division.

The Oilers still remain a potent team without a leader. If management is unable to find a replacement for the departed Moon, Oiler fans may have to wait a long time for that first Super Bowl victory.

Throughout his career, Warren Moon was one of the NFL's best quarterbacks.

Bud Adams

In 1959, Texas businessman K.S. "Bud" Adams formed the Houston Oilers. Adams loved football at an early age. He lettered in football at Menlo College and the University of Kansas.

In January 1961, with public money, Adams began building the Harris County Domed Stadium—also known as the Houston Astrodome. The stadium would feature "AstroTurf," a man-made turf created just for the Astrodome.

While the Astrodome was under construction, the Oilers played at Jeppesen Stadium, the local high school field. The Oilers won first place in the AFL Eastern Division three consecutive years and the league championship in 1960 and 1961.

In 1965 Bud Adams, center, spent one million dollars signing four tackles to the Houston Oilers.

Early Stars

The Oilers' early success hinged on the play of a few star players coach Lou Rymkus signed for his team.

Billy Cannon was a Heisman Trophy winner from Louisiana State University. The Oilers selected him in the AFL's first player draft. But the NFL's Los Angeles Rams also claimed Cannon. The case went to court. In June 1961, a judge ruled that Houston had the legal rights to Cannon, who then joined the team for its first training camp.

Coach Rymkus saw Cannon in camp and knew immediately he had a great player. In his three years with Houston, Cannon set season records in rushing, kickoff, and punt returns. He also led the AFL in rushing with 948 yards in 1961.

Safety/punter Jim Norton was a member of the Oilers' 1960 and 1961 championship teams, and a four-time league all-star. He held Oiler team records for career punts (519 with a 42.3 yard average) and career interceptions (45).

George Blanda was a quarterback/placekicker who had played for the Chicago Bears and Baltimore Colts from 1949 to 1958. In 1960, Rymkus signed Blanda. By the time he retired 15 years later, Blanda had set all-time NFL records for most games played (340), most seasons played (26), most points scored (2,002), and most points scored after touchdowns (943).

After playing for Houston for seven seasons, he signed with the Oakland Raiders in 1967. Blanda ended his long football career at Oakland in 1975.

A Roller Coaster Ride

Houston had much success in its early years. But from 1964 to 1980, the Oilers played inconsistently. Houston had eight losing years, seven winning seasons, and two seasons with .500 records. During that up and down time, they had seven coaches—and some great players.

Defensive end Elvin Bethea joined the Oilers in 1968 after an outstanding four-year college career at North Carolina A&T.

Bethea played a club-record 135 consecutive games with the Oilers until he broke his arm in 1977. Bethea also held NFL records for most games played, most seasons played, and most Pro Bowl appearances. Bethea led his team in quarterback sacks six different seasons.

Ken Houston's play was also impressive. But Houston's career got off to a slow start. Though his college team was a three-time national champion, pro recruiters paid little attention to him. Houston, a safety, was only a ninth-round draft choice. But he played 14 seasons, including 6 with the Oilers. In all, Houston caught 49 career interceptions. Even more, Houston made the Pro Bowl 12 consecutive times. He also held the NFL record for career interceptions returned for touchdowns. Houston was one of only two Houston Oilers inducted into Pro Football's Hall of Fame.

Quarterback Dan Pastorini was another star player. A first-round draft pick from Santa Clara, Pastorini played for Houston from 1971 to 1979. He threw for over fourteen hundred yards in nine consecutive seasons.

Opposite page:
George Blanda played quarterback and placekicker for the Houston Oilers.

Bum Phillips

Despite their talent, the Oilers did not do well until head coach O. A. "Bum" Phillips joined the team just three days before the 1975 college draft. From 1975 to 1980, Phillips led the Oilers to five winning seasons, two divisional titles, and two AFL championship games. His 55-35-0 record was the best in franchise history.

Bum Phillips was famous for his ten-gallon Stetson hat, snakeskin boots, and plaid western shirt.

Phillips wasted little time rebuilding the team. In the first round, he selected linebacker Robert Brazile of Jackson State and Texas A&I running back Dan Hardeman. Kansas wide receiver Emmett Edwards was chosen in the second round.

Brazile was an All-Pro choice his rookie year and from 1976 to 1982. He was known as "Dr. Doom" because he was hard to block. In 1975, Brazile, Hardeman, Edwards, and wide receivers Ken Burrough and Billy "White Shoes" Johnson helped the Oilers earn their first winning season in eight years.

Burrough caught passes for 1,063 yards and scored eight touchdowns. He led the team in receptions for seven years. Billy Johnson was a punt- and kickoff-return specialist. He led the team in both categories from 1974 to 1977.

With the help of these new players, Houston became one of the league's most promising teams. But in 1978, Houston became a contender when fullback Earl Campbell joined the Oilers.

Earl Campbell

Campbell, the 1977 Heisman Trophy winner from the University of Texas, was Houston's first-round draft pick in 1978. Despite his talents, Campbell did not dream of a football career.

Campbell grew up in Tyler, Texas. In his teens, Campbell took an interest in pool, cigarettes, and whiskey. After he was shot in the leg during a drunken brawl, Campbell dedicated his life to football.

Campbell was a great runner in high school and college. But he played even better in professional football as he became one of the NFL's most feared runners. For seven years, Campbell punished

Running back Earl Campbell glides away from Jets linebacker Lance Mehl.

Earl Campbell held all of the Oilers rushing records and was named to five Pro Bowls. Campbell still ranks as one of the NFL's leading rushers.

opposing tacklers with his powerful, bruising running style. When he left the Oilers in 1984, Campbell held all of Houston's rushing records and had been named to five Pro Bowls. He ranks as one of the NFL's all-time leading rushers.

With Campbell in the backfield, the Oilers captured two division championships in 1978 and 1979. Even more, they restored a winning tradition, posting winning records in 1975, 1977, 1978, 1979, and 1980.

A Super Gamble

In 1980, Bum Phillips took aim at the Super Bowl. He sent Pastorini to Oakland for quarterback Ken Stabler. Pastorini had been one of the team's most popular and consistent players. Stabler's career was waning. But he had won a Super Bowl title. Phillips hoped Stabler could help the Oilers win a championship.

Stabler proved himself as the season progressed. The Oilers finished with an 11-5 record and made the playoffs. But the Raiders and Dan Pastorini beat the Oilers 27-7.

After the game, Phillips said that Houston had been "outplayed and outcoached." Owner Bud Adams was furious with Phillips' statement and fired him on December 11, 1980—even though Phillips had led the Oilers to five straight winning seasons.

It was a bad decision. In the next four seasons, Houston had three different coaches. Even worse, Stabler left in 1981 and Earl Campbell struggled with injuries. The ground game and passing attack all but disappeared. Something had to be done.

Coach Phillips sent quarterback Dan Pastorini (left) to Oakland for quarterback Ken Stabler (right).

Jerry Glanville

At the end of the 1985 season, Oilers' assistant coach Jerry Glanville became head coach. Glanville set his sights on returning Houston to the playoffs. He wanted to turn the Astrodome into the "House of Pain."

Jerry Glanville was determined to turn the Astrodome into the "House of Pain."

Glanville had been a coach nearly all his adult life. A former linebacker for the Northern Michigan Wildcats, Glanville coached in Ohio high schools until 1966. The next year he was an assistant coach at Western Kentucky, where he also received his master's degree. Then in 1968, he joined Georgia Tech's Yellow Jackets as an assistant coach. Glanville's was also an assistant with the Detroit Lions, Atlanta Falcons, and Buffalo Bills.

Glanville's job was made much easier because the Oilers had recruited some new young talent to plug the gaps in both the Oilers' defense and offense.

From 1982 to 1984, Houston selected offensive linemen to improve their pass blocking and running game. In 1982, Penn State All-American guard Mike Munchak signed with the team. Throughout his professional career, Munchak was often named to the Pro Bowl.

With Bruce Matthews joining Munchak on the line, the offense reduced quarterback sacks by 50 percent. Matthews was an All-American guard from the University of Southern California and the number one draft pick in 1983. He started at all five offensive line positions as a professional.

In 1984, Houston's first-round draft pick was six-foot three-inch Dean Steinkuhler, one of the NFL's toughest offensive tackles. With Matthews and Munchak, Steinkuhler helped form a powerful offensive line.

Offensive Stars

Houston also improved its running and receiving game when wide receivers Drew Hill and Ernest Givins joined the team. Hill came to the Oilers from the Los Angeles Rams in 1985. He ranked first in club receiving yards in 1988. Hill and Givins combined for the most receiving yards in the NFL in 1987 and 1988.

In college, Ernest Givins played wide receiver, running back, quarterback, kick returner, and punt returner for the University of Louisville. He had a great rookie season in 1986 with over 1,000 receiving yards.

Oilers running back Mike Rozier cuts to his left as he tries to get around the Raiders defense.

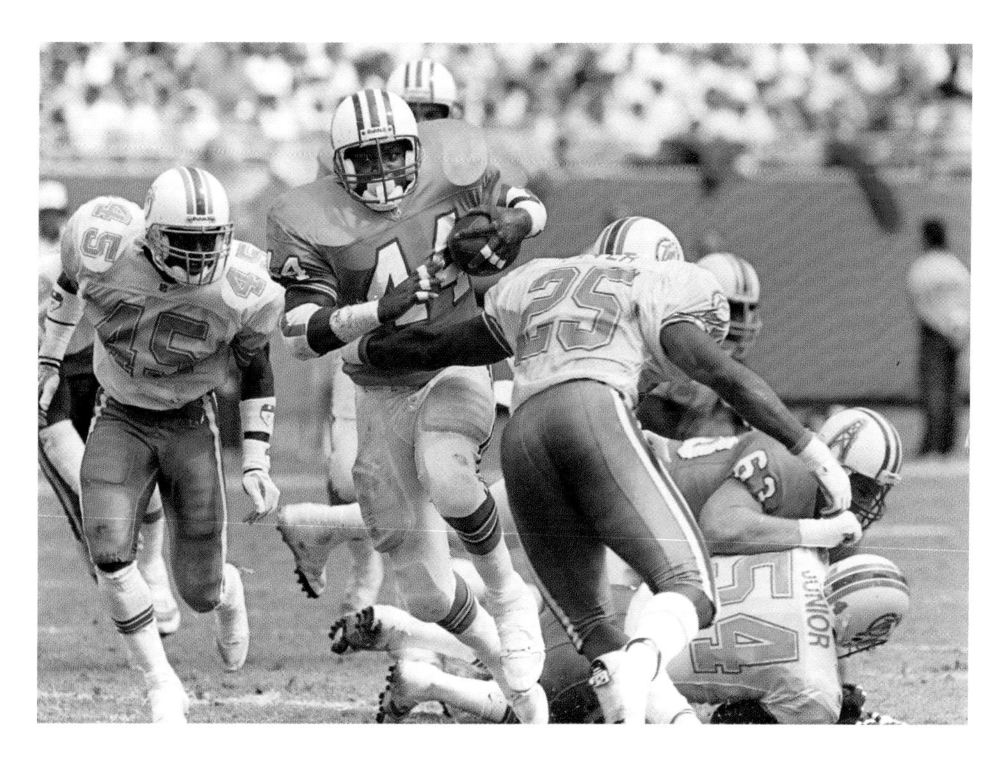

Lorenzo White was Houston's first-round draft choice in 1988.

The Oilers also drafted three good running backs: Mike Rozier (the 1983 Heisman Trophy winner), Lorenzo White, and Alonzo Highsmith.

Rozier played for the University of Nebraska. There, he set six Big Eight Conference rushing records. Rozier played in 1984 and 1985 with two United States Football League (USFL) teams. Houston selected him in the 1985 draft, and he quickly established himself. In his first four years at Houston, Rozier led the club in rushing, moving him into third place on the Oilers' all-time rushing list.

Lorenzo White, an All-American from Michigan State University, was Houston's first-round draft choice in 1988. Though he had limited playing time, White showed much promise.

Houston Oilers

George Blanda joins the Oilers in 1960.

Earl Campbell is the Oilers first-round draft pick in 1978.

Phillips leads the Oilers to five winning seasons from 1975 to 1980.

40 20 10

Lorenzo White is Houston's first-round draft choice in 1988.

Warren Moon, NFL's top passer in 1991.

Jerry Glanville leads the Oilers into the playoffs in 1988 and 1989.

40 30 20 10

Houston Oilers

Fullback Alonzo Highsmith could do everything—run, catch, and block. Highsmith was third in team rushing in 1988. Highsmith followed his father, an offensive lineman in both the NFL and the Canadian Football League (CFL), into professional football.

Perhaps the best offensive player for the Oilers was quarterback Warren Moon. In 1984, Moon followed Hugh Campbell, coach of the Edmonton Eskimos in the CFL, to Houston. Moon played six seasons for Edmonton. During the 1982 and 1983 CFL seasons, he passed for over 5,000 yards and scored over 30 touchdowns. In his first five years at Houston, Moon started every game and passed for over 14,000 yards and 78 touchdowns.

With these talented players, Glanville returned Houston to the playoffs in 1988. With Moon, Rozier, and wide receivers Drew Hill and Ernest Givins leading the way, the Oilers had one of the best home records. But they could not win on the road and had to settle for third place in the division. Still, their 10-6 record was good enough to get them into the first playoff round.

Houston traveled to Cleveland to play the Browns. The Oilers took a 14-9 halftime lead, but then fell behind 16-14 after three quarters. Lorenzo White's 1-yard touchdown run and Tony Zendejas' 49-yard field goal put the Oilers back on top 24-16. The Browns tacked on one more touchdown, but it wasn't enough as Houston held on for a 24-23 win.

In the next round, Houston faced the Bills in Buffalo. Because of the cold weather, the Oilers were a big underdog. But Houston played the Bills tough all the way before losing 17-10.

Oiler wide receiver Drew Hill jumps high to bring down a pass thrown by Warren Moon.

The following season, Houston finished 9-7, just one-half game behind first-place Cleveland. This time, the Oilers stayed home in the first playoff round to face the Pittsburgh Steelers. Houston hoped to use the home field to their advantage. But the game was tied 23-23 at the end of regulation. The Oilers then lost the game in sudden death when the Steelers kicked a 50-yard field goal. It was a bitter loss to fans and management. As a result, Glanville lost his job.

Jack Pardee

Coach Jack Pardee replaced Jerry Glanville. In 1990, Houston began the season with two straight losses. But once the run-and-shoot offense kicked into gear, Moon and receivers Drew Hill, Haywood Jeffires, Ernest Givins, and Curtis Duncan terrorized the league. Moon was on a pace to set a new league passing record when he dislocated his thumb in the 15th game. Backup Cody Carlson played well in the season-ending, must-win victory over the Steelers that put Houston into the playoffs. But the Oilers were blown out by Cincinnati 41-14.

Quarterback Warren Moon was on course to set new league passing records in 1990 before he dislocated his thumb.

The following season, Houston took no prisoners. With an 11-5 record, they won the Central Division outright for the first time ever and became the only team to make the playoffs every year from 1987 to 1991. But for the fifth straight year, they failed to get past the second round. The defense improved greatly, allowing the second-fewest points in the conference. The Oilers also put eight players in the Pro Bowl.

Opposite page: Houston Oilers coach, Jack Pardee.

Haywood Jeffries became only the fifth player in NFL history to reach 100 receptions in a season.

Moon was the NFL's top passer. He set league records for attempts (655) and completions (404). But he also tossed a career-worst 21 interceptions. Jeffires became only the fifth player in NFL history to reach 100 receptions in a season. But their second-round playoff loss to Denver left fans wondering if the Oilers would ever get to the Super Bowl.

In 1992, Houston earned its NFL-best sixth straight postseason appearance during an up-and-down season. The Oilers finished up the season without Moon who went down with an injury. Lorenzo White rushed for 1,226 yards and emerged as the starting running back. And with 90 catches, Jeffires led the AFC in receptions for the third straight year, while Givins led the AFC with ten touchdown catches.

The Houston defense was strong. It ranked No. 1 in the AFC and No. 3 in the NFL. The offense also finished second in the AFC. But the season ended in a nightmarish loss to the Buffalo Bills as the Oilers blew a 32-point lead against Buffalo in the first round of the playoffs.

The Oilers made the playoffs again in 1993. But the most memorable moment came in the playoffs when defensive coordinator Buddy Ryan threw a punch at offensive coordinator Kevin Gilbride during a nationally televised game against the Jets. Ryan and Gilbride had feuded all season, and coach Pardee was unable to stop it.

The Oilers started out 1-4, and Pardee's job was in trouble. But then the Oilers reeled off 11 straight victories to win the AFC Central. It was the longest winning streak in the NFL since 1972.

Ryan's defense was the league's best against the run and second in takeaways. Running back Gary Brown, who replaced injured White, rushed for 1,002 yards in the last eight games. The season was marred by tragedy when defensive tackle Jeff Alm committed suicide on December 14.

In the divisional playoffs against Kansas City, Houston jumped out to a 10-0 first quarter lead. By the end of the third quarter, the Oilers clung to a 10-7 lead. But then Joe Montana led the Chiefs to a 21-point fourth quarter explosion as they eliminated the Oilers 28-20.

Moonless

The fans were frustrated. And so was management. It seemed that the Oilers were stuck in a playoff rut. They needed big changes. So, after the season was over, Houston traded Warren Moon to the Minnesota Vikings.

Without Moon, the Oilers were a different team. They lost their 1994 opener to the Colts 45-21 as rookie running back Marshall Faulk rushed for 143 yards and three touchdowns against Houston's once-mighty defense. The Oilers waited until week four to notch their first victory, a 20-13 win over the Bengals. By week eight, the Oilers were 1-6. By week 11, they were 1-9. After the loss to the Bengals, Jack Pardee was dismissed as head coach. Pardee had taken the Oilers to the playoffs in each of his first four years. But the 1-9 record was too much for management to take. He was replaced by defensive coordinator Jeff Fisher.

But the slide continued. By week 16, the Oilers had fallen to 1-14. Their second win of the season came on the last day of the season with a surprising 24-10 victory over the New York Jets. But, oh, how the mighty had fallen. A year ago, the Oilers were in the playoffs. Now, they had one of the worst records in football.

Opposite page: Warren Moon in his Oilers jersey.

1

An Uncertain Future

The loss of Warren Moon proved devastating to the Oilers. Without their top passer and leader, the offense sputtered. Even the defense seemed to lose its fighting spirit.

It is all too clear to Houston fans that if the Oilers are to recapture their winning ways, they need a quality passer at the helm. Otherwise, it may be a long time before Houston finds itself contending for a Super Bowl.

GLOSSARY

ALL-PRO—A player who is voted to the Pro Bowl.
BACKFIELD—Players whose position is behind the line of scrimmage.
CORNERBACK—Either of two defensive halfbacks stationed a short distance behind the linebackers and relatively near the sidelines.
DEFENSIVE END—A defensive player who plays on the end of the line and often next to the defensive tackle.
DEFENSIVE TACKLE—A defensive player who plays on the line and between the guard and end.
ELIGIBLE—A player who is qualified to be voted into the Hall of Fame.
END ZONE—The area on either end of a football field where players score touchdowns.
EXTRA POINT—The additional one-point score added after a player makes a touchdown. Teams earn extra points if the placekicker kicks the ball through the uprights of the goalpost, or if an offensive player crosses the goal line with the football before being tackled.
FIELD GOAL—A three-point score awarded when a placekicker kicks the ball through the uprights of the goalpost.
FULLBACK—An offensive player who often lines up farthest behind the front line.
FUMBLE—When a player loses control of the football.
GUARD—An offensive lineman who plays between the tackles and center.
GROUND GAME—The running game.
HALFBACK—An offensive player whose position is behind the line of scrimmage.
HALFTIME—The time period between the second and third quarters of a football game.
INTERCEPTION—When a defensive player catches a pass from an offensive player.
KICK RETURNER—An offensive player who returns kickoffs.
LINEBACKER—A defensive player whose position is behind the line of scrimmage.
LINEMAN—An offensive or defensive player who plays on the line of scrimmage.
PASS—To throw the ball.
PASS RECEIVER—An offensive player who runs pass routes and catches passes.
PLACEKICKER—An offensive player who kicks extra points and field goals. The placekicker also kicks the ball from a tee to the opponent after his team has scored.

PLAYOFFS—The postseason games played amongst the division winners and wild card teams which determines the Super Bowl champion.
PRO BOWL—The postseason All-Star game which showcases the NFL's best players.
PUNT—To kick the ball to the opponent.
QUARTER—One of four 15-minute time periods that makes up a football game.
QUARTERBACK—The backfield player who usually calls the signals for the plays.
REGULAR SEASON—The games played after the preseason and before the playoffs.
ROOKIE—A first-year player.
RUNNING BACK—A backfield player who usually runs with the ball.
RUSH—To run with the football.
SACK—To tackle the quarterback behind the line of scrimmage.
SAFETY—A defensive back who plays behind the linemen and linebackers. Also, two points awarded for tackling an offensive player in his own end zone when he's carrying the ball.
SPECIAL TEAMS—Squads of football players that perform special tasks (for example, kickoff team and punt-return team).
SPONSOR—A person or company that finances a football team.
SUPER BOWL—The NFL Championship game played between the AFC champion and the NFC champion.
T FORMATION—An offensive formation in which the fullback lines up behind the center and quarterback with one halfback stationed on each side of the fullback.
TACKLE—An offensive or defensive lineman who plays between the ends and the guards.
TAILBACK—The offensive back farthest from the line of scrimmage.
TIGHT END—An offensive lineman who is stationed next to the tackles, and who usually blocks or catches passes.
TOUCHDOWN—When one team crosses the goal line of the other team's end zone. A touchdown is worth six points.
TURNOVER—To turn the ball over to an opponent either by a fumble, an interception, or on downs.
UNDERDOG—The team that is picked to lose the game.
WIDE RECEIVER—An offensive player who is stationed relatively close to the sidelines and who usually catches passes.
WILD CARD—A team that makes the playoffs without winning its division.
ZONE PASS DEFENSE—A pass defense method where defensive backs defend a certain area of the playing field rather than individual pass receivers.

INDEX